Artlist Collection
THE DOG
POSTER BOOK

SCHOLASTIC INC.

New York   Toronto   London   Auckland   Sydney

Mexico City   New Delhi   Hong Kong   Buenos Aires

ISBN 0-439-59370-0

4Kids Entertainment/THE DOG is a registered trademark of and © artlist INTERNATIONAL.

Published by Scholastic Inc.
SCHOLASTIC and associated logos are trademarks and/or registered trademarks of Scholastic Inc.

12 11 10 9 8 7 6 5 4 3 2 1   3 4 5 6 7 8/0

Designed by Carisa Swenson
Printed in the U.S.A.
First printing, November 2003

American Cocker Spaniel

Name
Cocker Spaniel

Type
Sporting

**First recognized by
American Kennel Club
(AKC)**
1885

**How tall are they (at
the shoulder)?**
14–15 inches

What do they weigh?
24–28 pounds

What are they like?
The Cocker Spaniel is the smallest member of the Sporting Group. It has a sturdy and refined head. Its long neck allows its nose to reach the ground easily. A Cocker Spaniel's coat is silky and flat, which allows for easy care. They are beautiful and very intelligent. You can always count on them to stay faithfully by your side.

DID YOU KNOW?
The Cocker Spaniel is one of America's favorite purebred dogs!

Basset Hound

Name
Basset Hound

Type
Hound

First recognized by AKC
1885

How tall are they?
11–14 inches

What do they weigh?
45–65 pounds

What are they like?
The Basset Hound is a short-legged dog with very long ears and droopy eyes. It has a narrow and long skull and is heavier in bone size than any other breed. Its smooth short coat is perfect for petting. The Basset Hound is a scenting dog; its keen sense of smell can lead it into all sorts of situations. It's best that you keep a close eye on this dog.

DID YOU KNOW?
Although Basset Hounds are low to the ground, they are pretty large in size. You'd need help lifting your Basset Hound.

Beagle

Name
Beagle

Type
Hound

First recognized by AKC
1885

How tall are they?
13–16 inches

What do they weigh?
20–25 pounds

What are they like?
These dogs are happy little tail-waggers! Beagles are curious and gentle and they love everybody. Beagles are squarely built with short coats in brown, black, and white. They always carry their tails upright.

DID YOU KNOW?
Beagle is thought to mean "small" in an ancient Celtic language.

Bulldog

Name
Bulldog

Type
Non-Sporting Group

First recognized by AKC
1886

How tall are they?
12–16 inches

What do they weigh?
49–53 pounds

What are they like?
A Bulldog is medium sized with wide shoulders and sturdy limbs. It has a heavy, thickset, short-faced head and a very smooth coat. Bulldogs are also very kind and courageous. They have a very dignified demeanor with a very expressive face.

DID YOU KNOW?
Bulldogs originated in the British Isles and are extremely sensitive to heat. They must be kept in an air-conditioned area with limited trips outside when the temperature is over 80 degrees Fahrenheit or the humidity is high.

Chihuahua

Name

Chihuahua

Type

Toy

First recognized by AKC

1904

How tall are they?

6–9 inches

What do they weigh?

2–6 pounds

What are they like?

The Chihuahua is a tiny dog with an apple-shaped head and a short, pointed muzzle. They have large dark eyes and ears that they hold erect. Chihuahuas are lively, bold, proud, and demanding of affection. They are very loyal—and will follow their owners everywhere. Don't tell a Chihuahua that it's too small to do something because it won't pay any attention to you!

DID YOU KNOW?

Some Chihuahuas weigh as little as 2 1/4 pounds, and some can even stand on all fours in a person's palm.

Dachshund

Name
Dachshund

Type
Hound

First recognized by AKC
1885

How tall are they?
There are three types of Dachshunds:

Standard: **Height: 14–18 inches; Weight: 20 pounds**

Miniature: **Height: up to 14 inches; Weight: 9 pounds**

Toy: **Height: up to 12 inches; Weight: 8 pounds**

What are they like?
Dachshunds can bring a smile to anyone's face. These little dogs with their happy smiles, bouncy walk, and long bodies just make you want to laugh. These dogs are lively, affectionate, and mischievous. Dachshunds like to bark—and their bark is very noisy—and they are compulsive diggers, so watch out for your garden!

DID YOU KNOW?
Dachshunds originated in Germany hundreds of years ago. *Dachs* means "badger dog," and dachshunds were originally bred to hunt badgers.

Dalmatian

Name
Dalmatian

Type
Non-Sporting

First recognized by AKC
1888

How tall are they?
19–23 inches

What do they weigh?
40–65 pounds

What are they like?
Dalmatians are spotted dogs that are strong and muscular. They are capable of great endurance and have an amazing amount of speed. Dalmatians are also very active and reserved.

DID YOU KNOW?
Dalmatians are born solid white and develop their spots later!

German Shepherd

Name
**German Shepherd
(also called Alsatian)**

Type
Herding

First recognized by AKC
1908

How tall are they?
22–26 inches

What do they weigh?
77–85 pounds

What are they like?
German Shepherds are strong, agile, and well-muscled. They are very alert and full of life. Most German Shepherds have black coats with tan or sable markings or they are all black. However, the dogs can come in many colors, including blue, liver and white, and even all white—but those are not standard colors and won't win in the dog show ring.

DID YOU KNOW?
German Shepherds have had many jobs: guard dog, police dog, tracker, search and rescue, drug sniffer, and guide for the blind.

Golden Retriever

Name
Golden Retriever

Type
Sporting

First recognized by AKC
1885

How tall are they?
20–24 inches

What do they weigh?
55–80 pounds

What are they like?
These dogs are well-mannered, intelligent, sweet, confident, and eager to please. They have feathered, medium-length, cream-to golden-colored coats, warm brown eyes, and long tails. They love to be around people and enjoy being around other dogs, too. Golden Retrievers have many talents, including hunting, tracking, retrieving, and narcotics detection. Because of their intelligence and desire to please, Golden Retrievers make great guides for the blind, therapy dogs, and service dogs for the disabled.

DID YOU KNOW?
Golden Retrievers love to swim!

Labrador Retriever

Name
Labrador Retriever

Type
Sporting

First recognized by AKC
1917

How tall are they?
21–24 inches

What do they weigh?
55–80 pounds

What are they like?
The Labrador Retriever is a strong, muscular, medium-sized dog. It has a clean-cut head with a broad back skull and powerful jaw. Its tail is very thick, tapers off at the tip, and is of medium length. The Black Lab has a short, weather-resistant coat that protects it from the water and harsh cold weather. They have kind, friendly eyes, and are very intelligent. They're the perfect companions.

DID YOU KNOW?
The Labrador Retriever is one of the prime breeds selected as guide and rescue dogs.

Poodle

Name
Poodle

Type
Non-Sporting

First recognized by AKC
1887

How tall are they?
There are three types of Poodles:

**Standard: Height: up to 15 inches;
Weight: 45–70 pounds**

**Miniature: Height: up to 15 inches;
Weight: 15–17 pounds**

**Toy: Height: up to 10 inches;
Weight: 6–9 pounds**

What are they like?
The Poodle has a very deep chest and walks tall and straight. Its neck is strong and long, which permits its head to be carried high and with dignity. Poodles love to exercise and are very assertive. They come in a variety of colors and sizes.

DID YOU KNOW?
Even though it is believed to have originated in Germany, the Poodle is the national dog of France.

Pug

Name
Pug

Type
Toy

First recognized by AKC
1885

How tall are they?
10–14 inches

What do they weigh?
14–18 pounds

What are they like?
All Pugs have square, thick-set bodies with large heads and dark, prominent (bulging) eyes. Pugs can be apricot, fawn, black, or silver in color, but it's not the color of their coats that makes them really distinctive. No, what really makes a Pug a Pug are the wrinkles on its face, which make it look worried or concerned. But these little dogs are lively and happy.

DID YOU KNOW?
The Pug has lived in the royal courts of Europe, in Tibetan monasteries, and in the Chinese court, and was even named the official dog of the House of Orange in Holland.

Rottweiler

Name
Rottweiler

Type
Working

First recognized by AKC
1931

How tall are they?
22–27 inches

What do they weigh?
85–130 pounds

What are they like?
The Rottweiler is a large, powerful dog with a roomy chest and a long, straight back. It has a large frame and is broad between the ears. Its tail is short and it has a coarse coat. Rottweilers are very confident, with a "wait and see" attitude. These dogs are strong and love to exercise. They're the perfect running mate!

DID YOU KNOW?
The Rottweiler is a powerful dog with a desire to protect its home and family.

West Highland White Terrier

Name
West Highland White Terrier

Type
Terrier

First recognized by AKC
1908

How tall are they?
9–12 inches

What do they weigh?
13–22 pounds

What are they like?
These little dogs are sturdy and compact, with a white coat—any other color is considered unacceptable in show rings. They have bright, dark, deep-set eyes and a penetrating gaze. These animals look like they are ready for anything, and they usually are. West Highland Whites love to be in the center of the action and aren't afraid to push their way in so that they don't miss a thing.

DID YOU KNOW?
West Highland White Terriers (also called Westies) were originally bred to help control the population of rats, foxes, and other vermin.

Yorkshire Terrier

Name

Yorkshire Terrier

Type

Toy

First recognized by AKC

1885

How tall are they?

6–7 inches

What do they weigh?

7–9 pounds

What are they like?

This longhaired toy terrier has a blue-and-tan coat that is parted on the face and down the spine, and falls straight down on either side of the dog's body. Don't let their small size and delicate appearance mislead you—Yorkies never notice these things. They love to have adventures and to get into trouble. But these dogs can also be demanding and need a lot of attention. And it takes lots of grooming to keep their coats in top form.

DID YOU KNOW?

Yorkies were originally bred for catching rats and for hunting badgers and foxes.